what I Saw™ in
Rocky Mountain

Text by Julie Gillum Lue   Photographs by Christopher Cauble

The Exploration of

_____

(Explorer, A.K.A. your name here)

_____ / / to / / _____

(Dates of exploration)

RIVERBEND
PUBLISHING

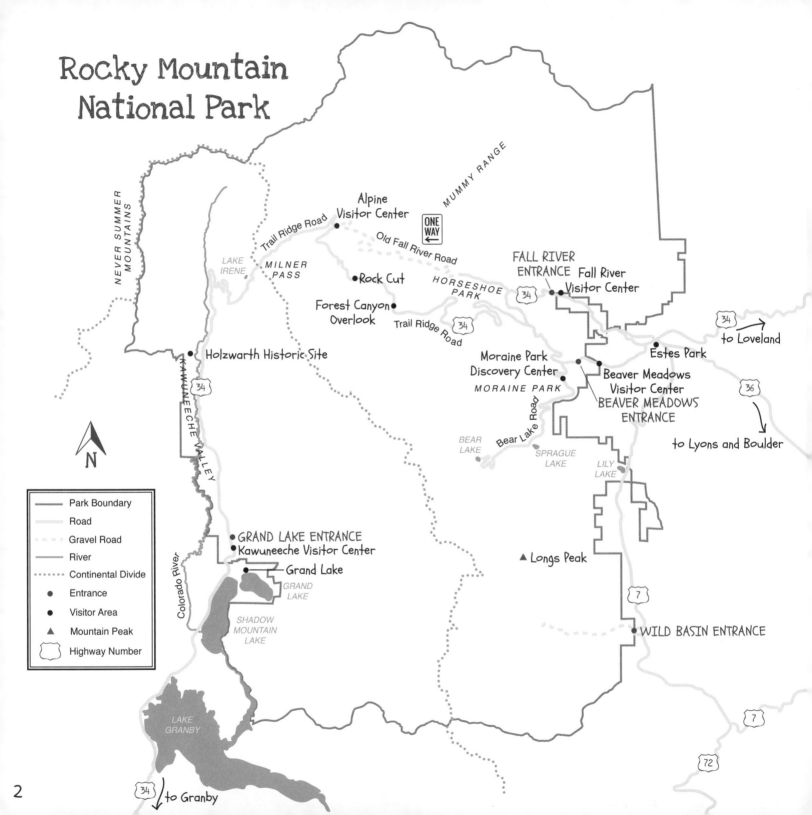

Rocky Mountain National Park

NEVER SUMMER MOUNTAINS

MUMMY RANGE

Alpine Visitor Center

Trail Ridge Road

ONE WAY ←

Old Fall River Road

LAKE IRENE

MILNER PASS

● Rock Cut

HORSESHOE PARK

FALL RIVER ENTRANCE

Fall River Visitor Center

34

Forest Canyon Overlook

Trail Ridge Road

34

to Loveland

34

● Holzwarth Historic Site

KAWUNEECHE VALLEY

34

Moraine Park Discovery Center

MORAINE PARK

Beaver Meadows Visitor Center

BEAVER MEADOWS ENTRANCE

Estes Park

36

Colorado River

N

BEAR LAKE

Bear Lake Road

SPRAGUE LAKE

LILY LAKE

to Lyons and Boulder

▬▬	Park Boundary
▬▬	Road
┈┈	Gravel Road
──	River
⋯⋯	Continental Divide
●	Entrance
●	Visitor Area
▲	Mountain Peak
⬡	Highway Number

● GRAND LAKE ENTRANCE

● Kawuneeche Visitor Center

● Grand Lake

GRAND LAKE

▲ Longs Peak

7

SHADOW MOUNTAIN LAKE

WILD BASIN ENTRANCE

LAKE GRANBY

7

72

2

34 ↓ to Granby

Contents

Introduction

If you come to Rocky Mountain National Park for the mountains, you won't be disappointed. The park is a high and rugged place, with so many mountains that some don't even have names. Almost 80 reach over 12,000 feet, which is more than two miles above sea level. The tallest of them all, Longs Peak, is a true "fourteener"—you may be able to guess what that means.

Reaching many of these mountain summits requires a strenuous hike or climb. But you don't have to climb a mountain here to stand on top of the world. A special highway called Trail Ridge Road winds all the way up to the alpine tundra,

Trail Ridge Road

where the weather is too harsh for trees to survive. In summer, surrounded by millions of tiny wildflowers, you can look down upon an amazing landscape.

Glaciers helped shape the park's peaks, valleys, lakes, and waterfalls. When the ice melted, it left behind post-card-pretty views. But these mountains offer much more than a beautiful backdrop. They provide homes for a huge variety of living things, from butterflies and bighorn sheep to pikas and ponderosas.

This area has been important to people for thousands of years. The Ute and Arapaho tribes used these lands for generations, hunting game and crossing the mountains on ancient trails. In the late 1800s, white settlers tried to make a living ranching and mining. But hard winters and poor mineral deposits left many disappointed. Homesteaders soon learned they could make more money taking care of summer tourists attracted by these high mountains and meadows.

As more settlers and visitors arrived, the wilderness became less wild, and overhunting wiped out the elk population. Some people started to worry about the area's future. Led by a mountain guide and innkeeper named Enos Mills, they lobbied for the creation of a national park. Rocky Mountain National Park was established in 1915 to preserve this special place for future generations—people like you. The park, often called "Rocky," now protects 415 square miles in northern Colorado.

What I Saw in Rocky Mountain National Park will help you learn about the some of the animals, plants, and places you are most likely to see when visiting. But if this book included everything you could find

Alpine sunflower

here, it might weigh more than you do! Some animals, like bears and mountain lions, are not described in the book because they are hard to see. Others, like great horned owls and porcupines, are nocturnal. This means they are active at night, when you are not.

Chickaree

As you travel through the park, see how many items in this book you can check off. But don't be disappointed if you can't find everything, especially the animals. The park is not a zoo. The animals roam where they please. If you don't see them, you can still learn about them, listen for their calls, and watch for their tracks or "scat" (a word biologists use for animal poop).

While you are exploring, ask your family to help you find answers to these questions:

★ Which animal eats mud to stay healthy?

★ What park feature is pictured on the Colorado state quarter?

★ What is the Arapaho word for "coyote"?

★ Which tree smells like dessert?

★ What is a hummingbird's favorite color?

The answers are in this book. But you will come across things that are not in this book, too. If you find a plant or animal you can't identify, take a picture. Bring it to a visitor center to ask a ranger or visit a bookstore, where you can find books on just about everything related to the park.

While having fun here, make sure you stay safe. Smart choices are your best defense against fast water, lightning, steep snowfields, wild animals, and other things that may hurt you. Please read the park newspaper for safety advice, including tips on hiking in bear and mountain lion country.

Here are a few rules you should follow to help protect you, the animals, and the park:

★ Keep your distance from wildlife. Rangers say if an animal changes its behavior because of you, you are too close.

★ Don't give any food to the animals. It's unhealthy for them and unsafe for you.

★ Leave flowers, plants, rocks, animals, and historic artifacts where they are.

Your best souvenirs are photos and memories, including the notes you make in this book. As you explore, maybe you'll be able to answer this question:

★ What is your favorite thing in Rocky Mountain National Park?

Elk

(Cervus elaphus)

Where to see them

In summer, you are likely to see elk above tree line along **Trail Ridge Road** or in the **Kawuneeche Valley** (May-July). In fall, watch for herds gathering in **Moraine Park**, **Horseshoe Park**, **Upper Beaver Meadows**, and the **Kawuneeche Valley**. In winter, many elk leave the park—you may even find them in town.

During the fall, you might hear an elk before you see it. The male elk, called a bull, "bugles" to challenge other bulls and let females know he is available for breeding. The bugle is a loud call that starts low and rises until it ends in a long, high-pitched squeal, often followed by several grunts. If another bull takes up the challenge, they may spar with their heavy antlers.

Like other members of the deer family, the males, called bulls, drop their antlers every winter and start growing them every spring. While a bull's antlers are re-growing, they are covered with "velvet"—a layer of skin and short hairs that is later scraped off. A pair of antlers from a grown bull elk can measure five feet across. Young bulls with skinny, unbranched antlers are called "spike bulls." Female elk, called cows, have no antlers.

Elk like to feed in meadows, but they go into forests to rest, hide, or take shelter from bad weather. They form different kinds of herds depending on the time of year. In summer, older bulls often form small herds of their own. Cow elk form larger herds with their spotted calves and other young elk. In the fall, the most dominant bulls guard groups of cows from other males.

When you see elk, stay back and use binoculars or a zoom lens to get a closer look. While you are looking, don't forget to listen, even in summer. Elk cows and calves "talk" to each other with squeals, barks, bleats, and other calls.

If you get confused about the difference between elk and deer, remember that elk are about twice as heavy as mule deer and have chocolate-colored heads and necks.

Cow elk

Guess what?

Another name for elk is wapiti, a Shawnee word pronounced WAH-pit-ee. It means "white rump," and when you see an elk you'll know why.

☐ I saw elk!

Where?

When?

How many?

What were they doing?

Bull elk

Mule Deer

(Odocoileus hemionus)

Where to see them

Mule deer roam throughout most of the park. Look for them along **Bear Lake Road** and in **Moraine Park**, **Beaver Meadows**, **Horseshoe Park**, and the **Kawuneeche Valley**.

Colorado has both white-tailed deer and mule deer, but if you see deer in the park, they are probably mule deer. Their common name refers to their oversized ears, which look like the ears of a mule. Mule deer are bigger than whitetails and have short tails with a black tip. The males, known as bucks, grow impressive antlers that branch out into forks and then divide again (like factor trees in fourth-grade math).

"Muleys" can gallop at around 40 miles per hour. But when they are startled, they often bounce away with all of their legs springing up and down at the same time, like a four-legged pogo stick: *boing-boing-boing*. This unusual gait, called

Mule deer buck

"stotting," is used to escape danger. In the park, deer have to be alert for predators (animals that want to eat them) like mountain lions.

Mule deer eat aspens and other trees, shrubs, grasses, flowering plants, and mushrooms. They are more likely to be out feeding in the morning and late evening. At other times of day, watch for their heart-shaped tracks in soft ground or the mud along streams.

You may find the tiny hoof prints of fawns mixed in with those of their mothers, known as does. Mule deer does often give birth to twins. Fawns are born without scent and covered with white spots to help them hide. If you find a fawn hiding in the grass, please leave it alone. Its mother will be back soon!

Guess What?

Mule deer are great jumpers. While stotting, they can cover 15 or 20 feet of ground with a single bound, and they can easily jump fences of six feet or more.

☐ I saw mule deer!

Where?

When?

How many?

What were they doing?

Where to see them

Coyotes are often seen in open areas like **Horseshoe Park**, **Moraine Park**, **Beaver Meadows**, **Hollowell Park**, and the **Kawuneeche Valley**.

Of the two kinds of wild dogs that still live in the park—coyotes and foxes—you are more likely to see a coyote. They are mostly active at night, but sometimes you can find them out hunting during the day, especially when they have hungry pups to feed.

Coyotes prey on voles, mice, ground squirrels, rabbits, and other small animals. When a coyote sees a mouse, it springs into the air and pounces like a cat. Coyotes also eat eggs, berries, and the carcasses of animals that have died over the winter. Sometimes they even team up with badgers when hunting ground squirrels.

An adult coyote is as tall as a medium-sized dog and weighs about 25 to 35 pounds. Coyotes usually have grayish-brown coats and big, bushy tails. When they run, they carry their tails low, as if they are trying not to attract attention.

In the spring, a coyote mother gives birth to four or more pups in an underground den. Both parents bring food to them until the pups are big enough to travel.

Coyotes can be quiet and stealthy while hunting. But they can also make a lot of noise, especially at night. They bark, yip, yowl, and howl. If you hear howling at night during your visit, you can be fairly sure it is a coyote, not a wolf. The last wolves in the park were killed about a hundred years ago.

☐ I saw a coyote!

Where?

When?

What was it doing?

Guess what?

You may pronounce this animal's name as a three-syllable word, kye-O-tee, or with two syllables, KYE-ote. Most people in this area say KYE-ote.

Bighorn Sheep

(Ovis canadensis)

Where to see them

Watch for bighorn sheep near **Sheep Lakes** in **Horseshoe Park** (often at midday), **Rock Cut**, and **Milner Pass**, and along the **Colorado River Trail**. In winter, also look for them along **Highway 34** outside the park's **Fall River Entrance**.

Bighorn sheep are about the size of deer, and the first thing you notice about them is their horns. Unlike antlers, horns are not shed each year. They look hard and bony, but they are made of something called keratin—the same flexible material as your fingernails. Female bighorn sheep, called ewes, have short, thin horns with a slight curve. The males, called rams, have heavy, thick horns that grow bigger every year. A 6- or 7-year-old ram has horns that curve around like a circle. Older "full-curl" rams sometimes rub off the tips of their horns on rocks so the horns won't block their view.

Rams' horns are not just for show. In late fall, rams use them to challenge others for a chance to mate with the ewes. Two rams charge at each other and slam their horns together so hard the loud, sharp "crack" sound can be heard a mile away. Thick, shock-absorbing skulls protect their brains.

Bighorn sheep have excellent eyesight. Their pupils—the dark parts in the center of each eye—are slitted, sort of like the pupils in cats and reptiles. But in bighorn, these slits look like rectangles turned on their sides. These strange eyes give sheep such good wide-angle vision they can almost see behind themselves.

Sheep avoid predators by escaping to the cliffs, where they feel safer. Their rubbery hooves give them good traction as they jump from one tiny foothold to another. But they are willing to leave the safety of the cliffs to visit mineral licks like those in Horseshoe Park. For bighorn sheep, eating the mud at Sheep Lakes is like taking a vitamin or mineral supplement. Ewes with lambs especially need calcium, one of many minerals contained in the mud.

Guess what?

Members of Rocky's "Bighorn Brigade" serve as crossing guards for bighorn sheep. On busy summer days, rangers and park volunteers stop cars near Sheep Lakes so sheep can safely cross the road.

Ewe

Ram

☐ I saw bighorn sheep!

Where?

When?

How many?

What were they doing?

Moose

(Alces alces)

Where to see them

Though moose sometimes visit the east side of the park (and have even been spotted swimming in **Bear Lake**), you're most likely to find them on the west side along the trails and in the **Kawuneeche Valley**.

Nothing else looks quite like a moose, with its long legs, horse-sized body, strangely shaped nose, and furry skin flap (called a "dewlap") hanging under its chin.

Like male elk and deer, bull moose grow antlers each year. But their antlers look very different. Scientists describe moose antlers as "palmate." Can you guess why? Each antler is shaped sort of like a hand.

Moose can run surprisingly fast—up to 35 miles per hour. Their long legs help them wade through deep snow and step over fallen trees in the forest. Moose also use their deadly hooves to defend themselves.

In summer, you are likely to find moose cooling off in a stream or lake. They can eat plants growing underwater by closing their nostrils. Moose are great swimmers and can even dive almost 20 feet to snag a tasty water plant. These plants are high in sodium, another name for salt. Moose crave sodium so much that in winter, they will even lick road salt off parked cars.

Unlike elk, moose don't form herds. You usually see a lone moose, or maybe a cow with her young. In the spring, a cow moose gives birth to one or two cinnamon-colored calves.

Watch for moose where you see water and willows, one of their favorite foods. It's exciting to see a moose, but if you do, remember to keep your distance. Moose can be dangerous if they feel threatened.

Guess what?

Moose are the park's largest animals. A bull moose can weigh 1,200 pounds.

Bull moose

☐ **I saw a moose!**

Where?

When?

What was it doing?

12

Where to see them

Watch for marmots at pullouts on **Trail Ridge Road**, including **Forest Canyon Overlook** and **Rock Cut**, and along **Old Fall River Road**.

Yellow-Bellied Marmot

(Marmota flaviventris)

If you've ever seen a groundhog or a woodchuck, the yellow-bellied marmot should look familiar. All three of these close relatives are super-sized ground squirrels. Each can weigh as much as a cat!

Though marmots also live in lower areas, they are most easily seen above tree line. You may find them romping across high meadows, lounging on boulders, or even trying to make off with your lunch. Please keep your food away from them so they can stay healthy and wild.

Marmots usually live in groups called colonies. Up to 20 marmots make their home together by digging a burrow under a rock pile. The rocks help protect the colony from predators and also make good lookout stations. A marmot on guard duty might sit upright on a rock as it keeps a close watch for intruders. When it senses danger, it will warn others with a high-pitched whistle.

During summer, marmots build up a thick fat layer to survive the coming winter. They mostly eat plants, but they will also eat eggs and insects. Marmots begin hibernating (sleeping through the winter) in September or October. A marmot heads underground, plugs its burrow entrance, and curls up with other marmots in a nest of dry grass. While it sleeps, its breathing and heartbeat slow down, and its body temperature drops until it's about as cold as the inside of a refrigerator. Marmots wake up in April or May, when more food is available.

Guess what?

Some people call marmots "whistle pigs" because of their warning calls, and possibly their eating habits.

☐ I saw a marmot!

Where?

When?

What was it doing?

Pika

(Ochotona princeps)

Where to see them

Pikas live in rocky alpine areas like those along **Trail Ridge Road**. They are often spotted near the **Tundra Communities Trail**, which begins at **Rock Cut**.

In the high country, when you hear something that sounds like a squeaky toy, look quickly. You might spot a pika disappearing into a rock pile. Wait patiently and it may reappear, ready for another food-gathering trip out on the meadows.

Though its closest relatives in the park are cottontails and snowshoe hares, a pika looks more like a guinea pig or extra-large hamster. Pikas have grayish-brown fur, rounded ears, and tails so small you can barely see them. An adult weighs about as much as a softball.

Despite their cuteness, pikas can be fierce when defending their territories from other pikas. But they still warn their neighbors with a high-pitched "beep" when predators approach.

A pika eating a leaf

Unlike marmots, which live in many of the same areas, pikas do not hibernate. They spend their summers cutting grass and flowers and piling them on rocks to dry. When this "hay" is fully cured, pikas stash it in their rock burrows to eat over the winter. If you see hay piles, you know a pika lives somewhere nearby.

Pikas are designed for cold temperatures—they even lived in this area during the last Ice Age. Because they overheat easily, they need places to live where summer temperatures are not too hot. But they also need good snow cover in winter to insulate their homes, so they won't get too cold. Snow protects pikas like snow caves protect mountain climbers.

Guess What?

Like their rabbit relatives, pikas have two sets of upper front teeth. The outer teeth are flat but sharp, like those of a beaver. The two inner teeth look like long, round posts.

☐ I saw a pika!

Where?

When?

What was it doing?

Chickaree

(Tamiasciurus hudsonicus)

If you get too close to a chickaree, it chatters loudly and lets out a squirrel yell that is hard to ignore. The chickaree is very territorial. Not only will it chase other squirrels that come too close, it will chatter at any intruder, including you.

Chickarees are also called red squirrels, but they look more brown than red and have a ring of white around each eye. They are fairly small and live mostly in the trees. If you see a large gray or black squirrel with tufted ears, you have found an Abert's squirrel instead. They spend their lives in and around ponderosa pines, like the ones near the Alluvial Fan or Aspenglen Campground.

Because chickarees don't hibernate, they must store food for the winter and keep it safe from other animals. They eat a variety of food but mostly rely on seeds from pine, fir, and spruce cones. Chickarees store their cones in piles called middens, which also serve as trash heaps for cones they have already chewed into bits.

☐ I saw a chickaree!

Where?

When?

What was it doing?

Guess what?
Chickarees can safely eat some mushrooms that are poisonous to humans.

Chipmunk

(Tamias species)

Where to see them

Chipmunks are often found along trails and at campgrounds, picnic areas, and turnouts. Watch for them at **Sprague Lake**, **Bear Lake**, **Moraine Park**, **Many Parks Curve**, and in the **Kawuneeche Valley**.

Unless you visit the park in the middle of winter, you'll probably come across a chipmunk or two. You might see one run across a road or scurry along a trail. Chipmunks are curious and sometimes approach people, but don't try to touch them or feed them. As cute as they are, chipmunks can bite or spread diseases.

Chipmunks are small members of the squirrel family. They are reddish-brown with long, bushy tails and thin, white-and-black stripes on their backs and pointy faces.

Chipmunks hardly ever sit still unless they pause for a snack. They eat seeds, nuts, berries, insects, and sometimes eggs or baby birds. When they find food that won't spoil, chipmunks stuff it into their fur-lined cheek pouches to carry back

PHOTO BY NPS

home. A chipmunk spends winter in its nest, saving energy by lowering its body temperature in a kind of light hibernation. It wakes up regularly to eat some of the food it has stored.

Guess What?

When alarmed, the chipmunk gives a sharp call that sounds like "chip"—a good bet that's how it got its name.

☐ I saw a chipmunk!

Where?

When?

What was it doing?

Where to see them

Look for golden-mantled ground squirrels in rocky areas, especially at **Sprague Lake**, **Bear Lake**, and **Many Parks Curve**, and in the **Kawuneeche Valley**.

(Callospermophilus lateralis)

You may have seen a golden-mantled ground squirrel without knowing it. Many people mistake these small, striped rodents for chipmunks. But you can easily tell the two species apart if you look at their heads. A chipmunk has stripes on its head and face, leading all the way to its pointed nose. A golden-mantled ground squirrel has no stripes on its head. The ground squirrels also are bigger and chubbier-looking.

Like chipmunks, golden-mantled ground squirrels pack food into their cheeks and haul it off to their burrows for storage. But they also eat enough to build up a thick fat layer. They spend the winter in hibernation and probably save most of their stored food for when they wake up in the spring.

Golden-mantled ground squirrels live in rocky areas in the mountains. They may "beg" for food from you, but please resist. Feeding ground squirrels harms them and ruins your chance to see them acting naturally.

☐ I saw a golden-mantled ground squirrel!

Where?

When?

What was it doing?

Guess What?

When they hibernate, golden-mantled ground squirrels lower their body temperature to near freezing.

Wyoming Ground Squirrel

Where to see them

Wyoming ground squirrels are often seen near the **Alluvial Fan** and in **Horseshoe Park** and **Beaver Meadows**.

(*Urocitellus elegans*)

In dry, open areas, watch for mounds of dirt marking the burrows of Wyoming ground squirrels. You might find these grayish-brown squirrels scampering around or standing next to their burrow entrances, watching for danger. They need to stay alert because they are eaten by many predators, including coyotes, foxes, badgers, hawks, and eagles. Sometimes, when one of them is hit by a car, it is even eaten by other ground squirrels!

Wyoming ground squirrels only see two seasons: spring and summer. They don't store food in their burrows. Instead, they store energy on their bodies in the form of a thick fat layer. They eat mostly plants, including some that are poisonous to other animals. After eating and eating until they store up enough fat, these ground squirrels hibernate for the rest of the year. They may start as early as August. If you walk through dry meadows in late summer, fall, or winter, think about the Wyoming ground squirrels sleeping somewhere below in their grass-lined nests.

Guess what?

Wyoming ground squirrels overheat easily. To stay cool in summer, they only spend about three hours outside their burrows each day.

☐ I saw a Wyoming ground squirrel!

Where?

When?

What was it doing?

18

Where to See them

Watch (and listen) for hummingbirds in flower-filled meadows, including those in **Moraine Park**, **Beaver Meadows**, **Horseshoe Park**, and the **Kawuneeche Valley**.

Broad-Tailed Hummingbird

(Selasphorus platycercus)

Broad-tailed hummingbirds chatter, but they don't really sing. Instead, the males play musical "instruments"—their wingtip feathers. The whistling or trilling you hear when a hummingbird flies overhead comes from these feathers brushing together at high speed. In summer, this sound fills the air from sunup to sundown as the red-throated males zoom around impressing females and chasing off competitors.

These hummingbirds spend their summers in the mountains, where a short growing season forces millions of flowers to bloom at the same time. They especially like to drink nectar from red, tube-shaped flow-

A male broad-tailed hummingbird
HUMMINGBIRDSPLUS.ORG

ers like skyrocket (scarlet gilia), red columbine, and paintbrush. The plants benefit, too, as tiny grains of pollen stuck to a bird's feathers get transferred from one flower to another. Broad-tailed hummingbirds also eat small spiders and insects. These serve as baby food for the tiny chicks, which each weigh about half as much as a paperclip.

For hummingbirds, nectar is like jet fuel, and they burn plenty of it. Broad-tailed hummingbirds spend about 15 hours each day feeding and searching for food. They survive cold summer nights by going into something called "torpor"—a kind of mini-hibernation in which their bodies get cooler and their heartbeats slow. When fall arrives, they head back to Mexico until the following spring.

Wildland firefighters report that hummingbirds like to buzz their red hard hats. If you wear a red hat or shirt, you might get buzzed by a hummingbird, too.

☐ I saw a broad-tailed hummingbird!

Where?

When?

What was it doing?

Guess What?

In the time it takes for you to say the word "hummingbird," a broad-tailed hummingbird's wings can beat 50 times.

19

Steller's Jay

Where to see them

Steller's jays gather where people do, at places like **Sprague Lake**, **Bear Lake**, **Hidden Valley**, **Many Parks Curve**, and **Farview Curve**.

(Cyanocitta stelleri)

What does a Steller's jay sound like? Almost anything it wants! Steller's jays squawk, rattle, and sing when they "talk" to each other. They also mimic the calls of other animals. In this area, sometimes a Steller's jay will imitate the call of the red-tailed hawk, a scary sound for many birds and other small creatures. With all the competition heading for cover, the jay doesn't have to share its food. If a real hawk enters the forest, a group of Steller's jays may "mob" it and keep up the harassment until the hawk flies away.

Steller's jays are mostly blue with black heads and triangle-shaped crests. They usually live in areas with conifers—trees that make cones, like pines, spruce, and fir. You might see a Steller's jay swooping from tree to tree in a picnic area or watching you curiously from a branch.

These smart birds don't migrate south in the fall, though sometimes they move to lower areas in bad weather. To survive, they collect food during the summer and bury it for the coming winter. They eat almost anything, including pine seeds, insects, fruit, eggs, and baby birds. They also watch squirrels, gray jays, and Clark's nutcrackers hide food, so they can steal it later.

Steller's jays often hang around campgrounds and overlooks, waiting for handouts. But please don't give them any. If young jays don't learn how to find food on their own, they may starve over the winter.

Guess What?

Sometimes Steller's jays even mimic the noises made by cats, squirrels, dogs, chickens, or sprinklers.

☐ **I saw a Steller's jay!**

Where?

When?

What was it doing?

Where to see them

Look for Clark's nutcrackers at **Many Parks Curve**, **Rainbow Curve**, **Sprague Lake**, **Bear Lake**, **Lake Irene**, and **Farview Curve**.

Clark's Nutcracker

(Nucifraga columbiana)

Many animals store food for winter, but Clark's nutcrackers are especially clever. Imagine stashing a winter's worth of groceries at over two thousand locations, in a "pantry" that stretches for miles. Could you find these items nine months later when they are covered with snow? Thanks to its extra-large brain, a Clark's nutcracker could easily locate them.

Clark's nutcrackers like to eat big, heavy seeds like the ones from limber pines. A nutcracker tears apart the cones to reach the seeds and stuffs them in a pouch under its tongue. Then it flies off to bury the seeds with its long, black bill. When winter comes and food is hard to find, it returns to fetch the seeds. Amazingly, the nutcracker will find almost all of them, probably by using landmarks. Seeds that get left behind can grow into a new forest.

Most birds don't nest until spring or summer, when there is more food available. But the nutcracker's food-storage strategy allows it to nest in late winter or early spring. Both parents incubate the eggs and take turns flying off to their seed caches to gather food.

Because limber pine seeds are too heavy to fly in the wind, the trees rely on Clark's nutcrackers to carry their seed to new locations. When you see Clark's nutcrackers fluttering about, enjoy watching them but make sure they don't snatch your food. They need to get back to important work—storing pine seeds and planting trees!

Guess what?

A Clark's nutcracker can bury 500 seeds in an hour.

☐ I saw a Clark's nutcracker!

Where?

When?

What was it doing?

Mountain Chickadee

Where to see them

Chickadees can be found in **Moraine Park**, **Glacier Basin**, **Endovalley**, **Aspenglen**, and the **Kawuneeche Valley**.

(*Poecile gambeli*)

Mountain chickadees are small, rounded birds with gray bodies and black-and-white heads. They live in pine and spruce-fir forests, where they pick through bark, needles, and cones to find food—often while hanging upside down.

In summer, chickadees act like tiny exterminators. They eat mostly insects, spiders, and caterpillars, including some that damage trees. But they also hide seeds to eat over the winter. Chickadees stay in the mountains year-round, though sometimes they visit lower areas in search of food. On cold mornings, they look like plush toys as they fluff out their feathers to stay warm.

When you walk through the woods, chickadees are quick to call out a warning. Some people think it sounds like their name: *chicka-dee-dee-dee*. Others think it sounds like the word "cheeseburger." If you look especially scary, a chickadee will add more "dee" sounds to the end of its call. But if you don't look like a threat, it might hop down to a lower branch for a closer look at you.

Even though mountain chickadees live in evergreen forests, they prefer nesting in aspen trees. They find a hole in an aspen and the female builds a fur nest. She also covers the eggs with fur when she leaves to grab a meal. If a squirrel or other animal tries to invade her nest, she will hiss like a snake and slap the sides of the nesting cavity with her wings.

Guess What?

Mountain chickadees that live at high elevations have bigger brains and are better at solving problems than their relatives that live at low elevations.

☐ I saw a mountain chickadee!

Where?

When?

What was it doing?

Where to See them

Look for dippers along the **North St. Vrain River** and at **Ouzel Falls**, **Chasm Falls**, the **Pool** (on the **Fern Lake Trail**), and **Adams Falls**.

American Dipper

(Cinclus mexicanus)

American dippers may not be flashy like tanagers or bluebirds, but they have an eye-catching talent—they can swim. These gray songbirds live along noisy mountain streams, where you may see one flying directly over the surface of the water or standing on a rock, bobbing up and down as it performs the dipper "dance."

Even when water is fast enough to be dangerous for humans, dippers dive right in. They use their long, strong toes to grip slick rocks as they stalk the stream bottom in search of aquatic insects (bugs that live underwater). A dipper stays warm in cold water under a coat of down and densely packed outer feathers. It keeps these feathers waterproof with oil from a gland near its tail.

Like beavers and river otters, dippers are equipped for swimming with their own version of nose clips and swim goggles. Special flaps keep water out of their nostrils, and clear inner eyelids help them see well underwater. Dippers' outer eyelids are covered with white feathers—you may catch a flicker of white when a bird blinks.

The dipper is sometimes called a water ouzel (pronounced OO-zul). This name is attached to several places in the park, including a creek, a waterfall, and a lake in Wild Basin. You may find dippers along Ouzel Creek or at Ouzel Falls. But don't bother looking for dippers at Ouzel Lake. Dippers don't spend much time around still water.

☐ I saw an American dipper!

Where?

When?

What was it doing?

Guess What?

Dippers sometimes build their nests behind waterfalls. They may fly directly through the spray to and from the nest.

Mountain Bluebird

Where to see them

Bluebirds can be seen in meadows and along their edges, especially in **Horseshoe Park**, **Moraine Park**, **Beaver Meadows**, and the **Kawuneeche Valley**.

(Sialia currucoides)

Mountain bluebirds wear the colors of the sky. Males are bright blue on top and lighter blue underneath. Females are mostly soft gray with just a touch of blue. In lower parts of the park, watch for them flitting across meadows or perching on fence posts and treetops.

Bluebirds nest in cavities—another name for holes. But unlike woodpeckers, they can't drill out new holes in trees. Outside the park, they often nest in birdhouses built by people who want to attract them. Inside the park, they nest in the hollow spaces of old aspens or ponderosas. They usually choose a nesting site with a good view of a meadow or other open area where they can hunt.

Bluebirds especially like to eat caterpillars, grasshoppers, beetles, and spiders. When hunting, they look more

PHOTO BY NPS

like tiny birds of prey than songbirds. They hover above the ground like miniature helicopters or even catch bugs in midair. But when they can, bluebirds watch from a fencepost or treetop and swoop down when they find something within range. They need to save energy, because after their eggs hatch, they will deliver food to their babies about a dozen times an hour.

During the breeding season, bluebirds are territorial. They won't allow other bluebirds to nest within a hundred yards or so. Once babies have grown, bluebirds will often join larger flocks in the fall.

Guess What?

Bluebird feathers do not contain any blue pigments. The birds look blue because of the way tiny air pockets in their feathers reflect light—something called "structural coloration."

☐ I saw a mountain bluebird!

Where?

When?

What was it doing?

24

Where to see them

Look for columbines at **Lily Lake**, along **Trail Ridge Road**, along the **Fern Lake** and **East Inlet** trails, and at **Holzwarth Historic Site**.

Colorado Columbine

(Aquilegia coerulea)

In the late 1800s, more than 20,000 Colorado kids voted in an election to choose the state flower. The Colorado blue columbine was the clear winner. It became the official state flower in 1899 and was later given special protection throughout Colorado.

The Colorado columbine is called blue, but its sepals (the outer parts of each blossom) range from pale-blue to lavender to deep purple. These flowers provide clues about the plant's pollinators. Each long, purplish spur that extends behind a flower holds a drop of nectar. This sweet juice can only be reached by hummingbirds, but-terflies, and insects with long tongues like hawk moths and certain kinds of bees.

In lower areas, Colorado columbines grow on moist hillsides, often under aspens. But these fragile-looking flowers are tough enough to survive above tree line when they find the right conditions. In the high country, the Colorado columbine often takes shelter near boulders.

On the park's west side, also look for red columbines, a special favorite of humming-birds. Sometimes you can find them blooming right outside the Kawuneeche Visitor Center.

☐ **I saw Colorado columbines!**

Where?

When?

How many?

Guess What?

All flowers—not just columbines—are protected in the park. They provide food for many animals, from hummingbirds and butterflies to pikas and bears. Enjoy their beauty, but please don't pick the flowers.

Paintbrush

(Castilleja species)

Where to see them

Paintbrush grows in sunny areas in a wide variety of park habitats. Watch for paintbrush and other wildflowers at **Hidden Valley**, **Milner Pass**, and the **Colorado River Trailhead**.

Many types of paintbrush grow throughout the park, from low valleys to high meadows. Each bloom looks like an artist's brush dunked in paint. Try to see how many colors of "paint" you can find. Red is common, but you also can find paintbrush in shades of pink, yellow, or almost white.

A paintbrush's colorful parts are not petals. These parts are called bracts, and they are more like leaves. A paintbrush's true flowers are hidden inside. The flowers, which look like tiny green tubes, hold nectar to reward hummingbirds and flying insects attracted by the flashy bracts.

When they don't have what they need to thrive, some species of paintbrush steal from their neighbors. Their roots reach out to the roots of nearby plants, which they use as a source of water, nutrients, and even toxic substances. When paintbrush attaches to the roots of silvery lupine, all parts of the paintbrush except its nectar and tiny green flowers become poisonous.

Guess what?

Paintbrush seeds are so small it takes hundreds of thousands to make up a single ounce.

☐ I saw paintbrush!

Where?

When?

How many?

26

Where to see them

Moss campion grows above tree line on the alpine tundra. Good places to look for tundra plants include **Forest Canyon Overlook**, **Rock Cut**, the **Alpine Visitor Center**, and **Medicine Bow Curve**.

Moss Campion

(Silene acaulis)

If you visit the high country on a windy day, you can see why moss campion keeps such a low profile. While taller wildflowers bob madly in the wind, "cushion" plants like moss campion stay snug in their gravel beds. Without leaving the trail, kneel down and hold your hand just above one of these plants. Does the air feel warmer?

Moss campion's tiny leaves are tightly packed to keep out the wind while trapping water and soil. In midsummer, each mossy-looking plant is dotted with pink flowers. Along with other low-growing wildflowers, moss campion forms a colorful carpet across the ground.

Moss campion lives in tundra areas throughout the Northern Hemisphere, including places like Iceland and Siberia. It can survive ferocious winds and harsh winters, but it can't survive being trampled. It recovers very slowly and may take decades to grow a few inches.

NPS Photo by Jacob W. Frank

While enjoying tundra plants, please stay on the trail, especially when you are visiting busy areas along Trail Ridge Road.

☐ I saw moss campion!

Where?

When?

How many?

Guess what?

To stay warm, moss campion clings to its old, dead leaves for insulation—for 50 years!

27

Alpine Sunflower

(Hymenoxys grandiflora)

Where to see them

Alpine sunflowers bloom mid-summer in tundra areas. You may find them near **Forest Canyon Overlook** or the **Alpine Visitor Center**, or along the trail above **Rock Cut.**

Alpine sunflowers stand less than a foot tall, but they still tower over most tundra plants. Instead of hugging the ground to stay out of the weather, they protect themselves like many animals do. To insulate themselves from wind and cold, alpine sunflowers wear "fur"—a covering of fuzzy-looking white hairs on their leaves and stems. They also turn their backs to the wind, which usually comes from the west here. Their large, yellow faces almost always look east, towards the sunrise.

Life is rough above tree line, so an alpine sunflower doesn't bloom every year. It grows only green parts and roots while it gathers strength. After several years of storing up energy, the alpine sunflower pops up its beautiful blossoms to attract pollinators. These bright, yellow-gold flowers are the biggest on the tundra. After flowers go to seed, the entire plant dies.

Guess What?

Because of its white hair, alpine sunflower is sometimes known as "old-man-of-the-mountain."

☐ I saw alpine sunflowers!

Where?

When?

How many?

Where to see them

Aspens grow in meadows and on mountainsides throughout the park. Fall colors are especially nice at **Hidden Valley**, from the **Bear Lake Road**, along the **Fern Lake** and **Cub Lake** trails, in the **Kawuneeche Valley**, and along the **East Inlet Trail**.

Aspen

(Populus tremuloides)

Aspens have smooth, whitish-green bark and bright green leaves that turn yellow-gold in the fall. Sometimes they are called "quakies" because of how their leaves quiver in a breeze. The stems of most tree leaves are round, but the aspen's leaf stems are flattened, like a circle squashed into an oval. When the wind blows, the flattened stem causes the leaf to tremble or "quake." See for yourself—blow gently on a leaf and watch it twist and turn. Aspen leaves are a little lighter in color on one side, making the fluttering more obvious.

Even though aspens produce seeds, most new trees grow as

sprouts from the roots of an existing tree. Sometimes all the aspen trees in a grove have grown this way. They are all parts of a single tree!

Aspen groves provide a place to nest for many birds and food for many animals. Elk and moose often eat the leaves and small twigs on young aspens. In winter, they scrape off the bark of older trees with their teeth, leaving dark scars on the pale trunks.

When there are many elk or moose in an area, it can be hard for aspens to survive. The fenced areas in meadows throughout the park are designed to keep large animals away from aspens and willows until they recover. Healthy aspens and willows will also help animals like beavers, which need them for food and building materials.

☐ I saw aspens!

Where?

When?

How many?

Guess what?

A grove of aspens that share a root system is called a "clone" or "clonal colony." In the fall, aspens in a clonal colony turn the same color at the same time.

29

Ponderosa Pine

(Pinus ponderosa)

Where to see them

On the east side of the park, ponderosas grow in many areas, including **Beaver Meadows**, **Moraine Park**, and **Horseshoe Park**.

Old ponderosas have heavy trunks that can reach over 100 feet tall. They are covered with thick, orange-red bark shaped like puzzle pieces. If you find one of these old trees, lean close and take a deep breath. What

do you smell? Many people think ponderosa bark smells like vanilla or butterscotch, especially in spring and early summer.

Young trees have flaky, dark-gray bark without much of a smell. All ages have long needles, which usually come in bundles of three.

Ponderosas grow in dry, sunny places at lower elevations on the park's east side. When you walk through one of these ponderosa forests, listen for the beeping of nuthatches, the drilling of woodpeckers, and the chattering of chickarees. Also, watch for much quieter Abert's squirrels, which build nests in the branches and munch on ponderosa twigs to survive the winter. These large, gray or black squirrels have long ear tufts that make them look a little like rabbits. Some people call them "squabbits."

Fire keeps the forest from getting too shady for ponderosas. Young trees and brush are killed, but old trees often survive. Their thick bark protects them from heat, and they usually have few lower branches to help fire climb into their crowns. But if fires get too hot, even the old trees can be killed.

Guess what?

Because ponderosas can live over 600 years, scientists often study their growth rings to learn about the past. Tree rings record dry and wet seasons and the history of fires in an area.

☐ I saw ponderosa pines!

Where?

When?

How many?

30

Where to See them

Lodgepoles grow from lower parts of the park up through subalpine areas. Look for them near **Glacier Basin**, **Sprague Lake**, and **Bear Lake**, and throughout the **Kawuneeche Valley**.

Lodgepole Pine

(Pinus contorta)

If you see a forest of tall, skinny conifers topped by clumps of branches, you're probably looking at lodgepole pines. When lodgepoles grow in a crowd with other trees, their lower trunks are mostly bare. But when they have plenty of space, they grow in more of a bushy pyramid shape with plenty of lower branches. To be sure you're looking at a lodgepole, check the tree's needles—the lodgepole is the only pine in this area with needles in bunches of two.

Lodgepole forests bounce back quickly after forest fires, even when many trees are killed. They drop pinecones full of seeds each year, but the topmost pinecones stay on the trees. These cones are sealed shut with sticky pine resin. When the heat from a fire melts the resin, these cones open up, spilling out their seeds. The fire burns out, but millions of lodgepole seeds lie on the ground. Many of these will successfully sprout into new trees.

In some parts of the park, most adult lodgepole pines have been killed by bark beetles. On dead and dying trees, the needles turn from green to red before falling off. These trees have been cut down in areas like Glacier Basin and Timber Creek campgrounds to keep people safe. But many dead trees are still standing throughout the park. In windy weather, make sure you stay away from dead trees, because they can fall without warning.

☐ I saw lodgepole pines!

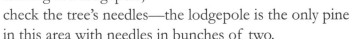

Where?

When?

How many?

Guess what?

Native Americans in the Rocky Mountains used—and sometimes still use—poles from lodgepole pines for their tipis, or lodges. That's why these trees are called lodgepole pines.

Engelmann Spruce

(Picea engelmannii)

Where to see them

Look for Engelmann spruce in subalpine areas like **Bear Lake**, **Hidden Valley**, **Lake Irene**, and **Farview Curve**. You can see krummholz along **Trail Ridge Road** above **Rainbow Curve** on the east side, and between **Medicine Bow Curve** and **Milner Pass** on the west side.

Engelmann spruce live in cool, moist areas with plenty of snow. When conditions are right, these trees grow tall and pointy, in the shape of upside-down ice cream cones. But Engelmann spruce look very different when they live near tree line (the limit beyond which trees can't survive). Sometimes a tree has branches only on one side, pointing away from the strongest winds. These trees are called flag trees. As you head up towards the tundra, you also will find trees that look more like shrubs creeping along the ground. These brushy trees are called krummholz, a German word that translates to "twisted wood." They grow slowly and are constantly pruned back by wind and bad weather. These trees are very short, often no higher than your knees. But one with a trunk as big around as your arm can be over 300 years old.

Along with subalpine fir and limber pine, Engelmann spruce dominate the subalpine forest—all those miles of dark green you see looking down from Trail Ridge Road. Many people think spruce and fir look alike, but up close, you can easily tell the difference. Engelmann spruce trees have pinkish-gray, scaly-looking bark. Subalpine firs have smooth, pale-gray trunks covered with little swellings. Both trees have short needles, but spruce needles are square and sharp. Fir needles are flat and soft.

Guess What?

Some Engelmann spruce trees at Hidden Valley (near Junior Ranger Headquarters) are over 600 years old. They sprouted before the year 1400!

☐ I Saw Engelmann Spruce!

Where?

When?

How many?

Where to see it

The peak is visible from many places on the east side of the park, including the **Beaver Meadows Visitor Center** and **Moraine Park Discovery Center**, **Trail Ridge Road**, and the north side of **Bear Lake**. You can get a closer look from Highway 7 near the turnoff for the **Twin Sisters Trailhead**.

Longs Peak is the park's highest mountain and one of Colorado's most recognizable peaks. Its summit rises 14,259 feet above sea level (about two-and-a-half miles). You can even see it from Denver, or as far north as the Wyoming border.

The mountain gets its name from Stephen Long, an Army explorer who traveled through this area in 1820. But American Indians knew Longs Peak and nearby Mount Meeker as the "two guides." If you learn to identify Longs Peak, you can use it as a landmark, too.

Glaciers helped carve Longs Peak's unique shape, including the "Diamond," a 1,000-foot wall of pinkish-gray granite on the mountain's east face. But glaciers didn't touch the peak's summit. The top of Longs Peak is almost flat and covered with broken slabs of rock.

Thousands of people try to climb Longs Peak each year. Most take the easiest way to the top, the Keyhole Route. But even this route is tough and dangerous. The distance to the summit is almost eight miles, and the last mile-and-a-half requires scrambling across scary ledges where there is no trail. Only bulls-eyes painted on the rocks mark the way.

More difficult routes on the mountain attract expert technical climbers. Many test their skills on the Diamond. They use ropes and other equipment to stay safe as they scale impossible-looking cliffs, often using tiny handholds or footholds.

U.S. quarter showing Longs Peak

☐ I saw Longs Peak!

When?

What was it like?

Guess What?

You might have a picture of Longs Peak in your pocket. The mountain's image is embossed on the 2006 Colorado state quarter.

Bear Lake

Where to see it

The lake is at the end of **Bear Lake Road**, which begins near the **Beaver Meadows Entrance**. To avoid the busiest times, try visiting on a weekday, or early or late in the day. In summer, you can take a free shuttle bus from several locations to the **Bear Lake Parking Lot**, which usually fills very early in the morning.

Out of about 150 lakes in the park, Bear Lake is the most popular. Many people walk the half-mile loop around the lake or start here for longer hikes.

Glaciers are responsible for much of the landscaping at Bear Lake. They formed when snow piled deeper every year until its own weight squashed it into glacial ice. Then the ice started to flow downhill, like slow but very powerful rivers. As they moved, glaciers whittled down the sides of the mountains, including pointy-looking Hallett Peak. They gouged out U-shaped valleys and excavated pits like the one that holds Bear Lake. Along their sides and front edges, they left ridges of dirt and rock called moraines.

While walking around the lake, notice the different kinds of rocks dumped here by glaciers. The speckled rocks are called granite and the stripy-looking rocks are called gneiss (pronounced NICE) and schist. If you can't find granite nearby, look up. From the north side of the lake, you can see a huge chunk of granite—Longs Peak.

In the Bear Lake area, you may see many small animals like chipmunks, ground squirrels, jays, and nutcrackers. Please help them stay wild by not feeding them. In early summer, look for greenback cutthroat trout spawning (laying eggs and fertilizing them) where the creek flows into the lake. These beautiful native fish have pinkish-red slashes on their throats and hundreds of dark spots on their backs and sides.

Guess What?

There are only 20 to 25 bears in the park, so you probably won't see any at Bear Lake.

☐ I Saw Bear Lake!

When?

What was it like?

Horseshoe Park is a large meadow surrounded by mountains, including the high peaks of the Mummy Range. In the western United States, places like this are often called "parks." You may have already seen Moraine Park and Estes Park, which is also the name of a town. Mountain parks are a good place to look for elk in the fall, when they gather in large herds for the "rut" (mating season).

The "horseshoe" part of Horseshoe Park's name comes from the squiggly path of Fall River. It winds back and forth in horseshoe shapes across the meadow.

A horseshoe-shaped bend on Fall River

PHOTO BY JULIE LUE

In summer, Horseshoe Park is covered with grass and wildflowers. But it was once covered with ice 500 feet thick—about the height of a 50-story building. Glaciers flowed down the mountains and buried the valley floor. When the glaciers started to melt, dirt and rock buried blocks of ice, leaving behind holes that would later become Sheep Lakes.

About a mile west of Sheep Lakes, the Alluvial Fan shows how the earth can change much more quickly. In 1982, a dam failed high in the mountains at Lawn Lake. More than 200 million gallons of water charged down the Roaring River towards Fall River and Estes Park. The flood created a temporary lake named Fan Lake. It also left behind a pile of rocks and dirt big enough to fill 30,000 dump trucks. Flooding struck this area and the rest of the park's east side again in 2013.

Guess What?

When the Lawn Lake Dam failed, the Roaring River really roared. According to the garbage truck driver who first reported the flood, it sounded "like a jet had crashed into the mountain."

☐ I Saw HorseShoe Park!

When?

What was it like?

Trail Ridge Road

Where to see it

Trail Ridge Road is the main park highway linking **Estes Park** on the east and **Grand Lake** on the west. It closes for winter and may also close temporarily at other times because of weather. Take shelter in your car or the visitor center during thunderstorms. Also stay off steep snowfields.

Trail Ridge Road takes you to a different world and back again. Whether you start driving at Grand Lake or Estes Park, you will climb about 4,000 feet, to a high point of 12,183 feet. At the top, you will find different plants and animals, different weather, and even different air. The air contains less oxygen—the stuff you need to stay alive—and is much colder. The temperature may drop three to five degrees for each 1,000 feet you climb.

The road was finished in the 1930s, but it follows a route used by people to cross the mountains long before cars were invented. Some spear points found nearby are over 10,000 years old! Near the top is the Alpine Visitor Center, the highest visitor center in a U.S. national park. It's also the end point for Fall River Road, a one-way dirt road that begins near Horseshoe Park.

Trail Ridge Road climbs through three life zones, which you can tell apart by the trees. The montane zone, up to about 9,500 feet, is dominated by ponderosas on the east side and lodgepoles on the west. The subalpine zone contains more fir and spruce, which grow shorter and more twisted as you gain altitude. The alpine zone, starting at about 11,500 feet, has no trees at all. In summer, the alpine tundra is covered with amazing wildflowers. The tundra also provides a home for pikas, marmots, and well-camouflaged birds called ptarmigan (pronounced with a silent "p").

Like many mountaintops in the park, the upper section of Trail Ridge looks like a gently sloping plain. While it was still low, this plain was worn nearly flat by erosion—forces like wind and water. It was lifted up when the Rocky Mountains started to rise. This area was above the reach of the glaciers that shaped so much of the park.

Guess What?

Winter winds on Trail Ridge can blow at 150 miles per hour, piling snow in drifts over 20 feet high. In spring, it takes about six weeks for rotary snowplows, graders, and bulldozers to open the road.

☐ I Saw Trail Ridge Road!

What part?

When?

What was it like?

Continental Divide

Where to see it

You can drive across the Continental Divide at **Milner Pass**. You can see the mountains of the Divide from almost anywhere in the park, with especially nice views from **Sprague Lake**, **Forest Canyon Overlook**, **Rock Cut**, and the **Gore Range Overlook**.

On the park map, look for a dotted line that divides the park roughly in two, from south to northwest. This line marks the Continental Divide. When rain falls or snow melts on the west side of this Divide, it flows towards the Pacific Ocean. On the east side, it flows towards the Atlantic. If you stand directly on the Divide and pour a little from your water bottle, who knows?

In this area, the Continental Divide is formed by a high ridge of mountains. These mountains are made of ancient rocks that started to rise millions of years ago, when giant pieces of the earth's crust, called tectonic plates, got shoved together. Much later, during the Ice Age, glaciers carved out the details.

In the park, the west and east sides of the Continental Divide have slightly different climates. The west side is wetter, colder, and not as windy. It gets more snow but no longer has any glaciers. The east side is drier, not as cold, and much windier. These winds have helped keep alive a handful of small glaciers left over from the "Little Ice Age," which ended less than 200 years ago. (You can see Tyndall Glacier from Sprague Lake.) Wind piles snow in drifts so deep they survive the heat of summer. Though small compared to Alaskan glaciers, the park's glaciers (including rock glaciers) contain about the same amount of water used by the city of Denver in two years.

Poudre Lake at Milner Pass on the Continental Divide

Guess what?

The Continental Divide, also known as the Great Divide, doesn't end at park, state, or national boundaries. It stretches from the Bering Strait in Alaska to the Strait of Magellan in Chile.

☐ I saw the Continental Divide!

Where?

When?

What was it like?

Where to see it

Trail Ridge Road runs directly through the **Kawuneeche Valley** on the west side of the park. To see the valley from above, stop at **Farview Curve**.

The Kawuneeche Valley is a large, marshy valley on the park's west side. During the Ice Age, this valley was covered by a glacier 20 miles long and more than a quarter-mile thick. Now it's a great place to spot wildlife and view the Colorado River near its source. Many trails lead from the valley into the high meadows, lakes, and mountains above.

The mountains just west of the valley are called the Never Summers. These mountains are the leftovers of volcanoes that eroded away, leaving behind their magma chambers. Four of them are named after types of clouds—Cirrus, Cumulus, Nimbus, and Stratus. Two others are named Thunder Mountain and Static Peak. These names might give you a few clues about the weather here. In the late 1800s, miners tried their luck mining for silver in the Never Summers and on Shipler Mountain. But within a few years, the boom went bust and they moved on.

If you spend much time on the west side, you probably will learn several words in the Arapaho language. Tonahutu means "big meadows," Onahu means "horse warms himself," and Kawuneeche means "coyote." "Never Summer" is also a translation from Arapaho. American Indian names are a good reminder that people lived and hunted here long before the national park was created. The Ute used this area and the rest of the park for over a thousand years. Later, these lands also became important to the Arapaho.

I saw the Kawuneeche Valley!

When?

What was it like?

Guess What?

The Kawuneeche Valley is named after a coyote, but these days you are just as likely to see a moose. Moose moved in during the 1980s after being transplanted to an area west of the park.

Holzwarth Historic Site

Where to see it

The historic site is located in the **Kawuneeche Valley** just south of **Timber Creek Campground**, about eight miles north of the **Grand Lake Entrance**. From the parking lot, it's an easy half-mile walk.

At Holzwarth Historic Site, you can imagine what it was like to take a vacation here in the early 1900s. John and Sophia Holzwarth were German immigrants who homesteaded this land in 1917, before the Kawuneeche Valley became part of the park. They started out raising cattle and growing hay. But ranching in such a high valley was a hard way to make a living. After dealing with some especially troublesome houseguests, they decided to charge overnight visitors. By 1920, the Holzwarths and their teenage children had turned their working ranch into the Holzwarth Trout Lodge.

For two dollars a day, guests could stay at the lodge, go hunting and fishing, ride horses, and eat Sophia's home cooking. They had cookouts and campfires, listened to stories, and helped with ranch work like chopping wood or herding cattle. The lodge became so popular that sometimes people had to sleep outside. After about ten years, the Holzwarths expanded by opening the Never Summer Ranch. These lands became part of the park in 1975.

The Holzwarth Historic Site still preserves a taxidermy shop, an ice house, a wood shed, and several cabins. In summer, you may be able to catch a tour through the "Mama Cabin." Here, on a stove named "Admiral Blue," Sophia cooked trout, wild game, breads and cakes, and German dishes like liver dumplings.

Guess What?

The Holzwarth Trout Lodge was one of many private lodges and tourist businesses scattered throughout Rocky in the park's early days. There was even a golf course in Moraine Park.

☐ I saw Holzwarth Historic Site!

When?

What was it like?

Where to see it

The river begins near **La Poudre Pass** in the park's backcountry. You can see lower sections of the river from **Holzwarth Historic Site** and the **Coyote Valley Nature Trail**. The river is also visible at a distance from **Farview Curve**.

At its birthplace in the Never Summer Mountains, the Colorado River looks more like a trickle. It is so small a hiker can step across it! But it grows quickly as it flows through the Kawuneeche Valley and is joined by other streams.

The river attracts many kinds of wildlife. It draws moose, otters, and birds, including ospreys—large birds of prey that dive in the water to catch fish. Non-native fish, especially brook trout, now dominate the river. But Colorado River cutthroat trout, which have lived here thousands of years, can still be found in the river and many lakes and creeks that feed into it.

In the park, some of the water headed for the Colorado River gets rerouted by the Grand Ditch and sent to the east side of the Continental Divide. Digging began on the Grand Ditch in the 1890s, before the

surrounding area became a national park. The Grand Ditch looks like a slash across the mountains west of the Kawuneeche Valley.

After the Colorado leaves the park, it eventually grows into a powerful river that roars through the Grand Canyon. It will travel more than 1,400 miles, providing water for over 30 million people and millions of acres of crops. But by the time the Colorado River nears the Pacific Ocean, almost all of its water will have been used up. Once again, the river will become a trickle, or even disappear.

☐ I saw the Colorado River!

When?

What was it like?

Guess what?

Until 1921, the Colorado River in this area was known as the Grand River—a name still attached to places like Grand County, Grand Lake, and the Grand Ditch.

I Met a Park Ranger!

Have you ever wondered what it's like to be a ranger? Rangers who work in national parks are called park rangers, not forest rangers. You usually find them wearing the National Park Service uniform of green pants and a gray shirt with a brown arrowhead patch on the sleeve. Some rangers have very specialized jobs, but others do a bit of everything. Many of them have special training to help people who are sick, hurt, or lost.

The easiest way to meet a ranger is to stop by a visitor center or attend a ranger-led program. Rangers

A park ranger teaching a "junior ranger" NPS PHOTO

called interpreters or naturalists offer walks, talks, hikes, and campfire programs that help you learn about everything from glaciers to bighorn sheep. Ask about programs specially designed for kids. You can find schedules in the park newspaper, at visitor centers, or on the park's website at www.nps.gov/romo.

While traveling through the park, you may run into other kinds of rangers, too. Law enforcement rangers are like police officers, except that they also manage things like "elk jams"—traffic jams caused when people stop to see elk! Backcountry

Guess What?

Even though Smokey Bear is the symbol for the U.S. Forest Service, Smokey and National Park Service rangers wear the same kind of hats. Rangers call them "flat hats." Sometimes you see rangers wearing different kinds of hats that are more practical for working outside.

Park ranger's hat

rangers hike the trails, keep backcountry campsites clean, and sometimes help rescue people. The park also has many other employees that do important work like fighting wildfires, maintaining roads and trails, researching the park's plants and animals, taking care of buildings, and protecting historic sites.

You can have fun learning about the park while earning a junior ranger badge. Pick up a junior ranger booklet for your age group at any park visitor center or at Junior Ranger Headquarters, which is open during the summer in Hidden Valley. Complete the activities,

Rangers can teach you about moose and other park wildife.

and when you are finished, bring the booklet back to a visitor center. Who knows? Maybe you will be a park ranger someday!

☐ **I met a park ranger!**

Ranger's Autograph:

Where:

When:

I Took a Hike!

Hiking is a great way to get exercise while exploring parts of the park you can't see from the roads. It also gives you a chance to notice things like flowers, rocks, feathers, tracks, and tiny wildlife like insects or toads.

Before you go, check the weather and read the park newspaper for safety advice, including information about lightning, bears, and mountain lions. Talk to a ranger if you have questions. Load your pack with water, snacks, rain gear, an extra layer, and a trail map. If you are hiking in the high country, start early and make sure you are not above tree line in a thunderstorm. While hiking, stay close to your group—don't run ahead, fall behind, or hike by yourself between groups. Check your map at intersections so you don't get lost. Keep back from steep drop-offs, waterfalls, and fast water.

If your group hasn't hiked before, start with a short walk or two and work up to longer hikes as you get used to high elevations. You probably already know about the short loop trail around Bear Lake. Here are a few other options:

Guess What?

There are 355 miles of trails in the park.

Sprague Lake

Distance and Location: .9-mile loop around lake starting at Sprague Lake Picnic Area.

This easy, wheelchair-accessible trail takes you around a lake that reflects the Continental Divide. Abner Sprague built this lake so guests at his lodge would have a place to fish. Watch for ducks, brook trout, and maybe even a muskrat.

Adams Falls

Distance and Location: .6-mile roundtrip from the East Inlet Trailhead near Grand Lake.

At the waterfall, watch for dippers but stay back from the edge. Continue up the trail past the falls for great views of a meadow and mountain valley.

PHOTO BY JULIE LUE

Dream Lake

Distance and Location: 2.2-mile roundtrip from Bear Lake.

This popular trail takes you to a subalpine lake with views of the mountains. For a longer hike, continue .7 miles up the trail to Emerald Lake.

Cub Lake

Distance and Location: 4.6-mile out and back hike from the Cub Lake Trailhead in Moraine Park.

This trail leads to a shallow lake covered with lily pads. Along the lower part of the trail, you will find many glacial erratics—boulders carried here by glaciers. The trail also offers a chance to see wildflowers and many kinds of small animals like birds, ground squirrels, marmots, garter snakes, and weasels.

Coyote Valley

Distance and Location: 1-mile roundtrip beginning from the Coyote Valley Trailhead in the Kawuneeche Valley.

Learn about riparian (streamside) areas as you walk a flat trail along the Colorado River. Elk are sometimes spotted in the meadow. This trail is also wheelchair accessible.

☐ **I took a hike!**

Where?

How far did you hike?

What did you see?

More Things I Saw Checklist

Rocky Mountain National Park has over 60 species of mammals, 280 species of birds, more than 1,000 species of plants, and so many special places you could not visit them all in a lifetime. Some of them are described in this book, and you may have already checked them off. But here is a checklist of some other animals and places you may see in the park. There is also a space for writing about things not in this book. Good luck and have fun!

Mammals
- [ ] Abert's squirrel
- [ ] Mountain cottontail
- [ ] Muskrat
- [ ] Badger
- [ ] River otter
- [ ] Marten
- [ ] Red fox
- [ ] Porcupine
- [ ] Black bear

Red fox

Places
- [ ] Lily Lake
- [ ] Wild Basin
- [ ] Moraine Park
- [ ] Fall River Road
- [ ] Alpine Visitor Center
- [ ] Never Summer Mountains

Lily Lake

Red-winged blackbird

Fish and Reptiles
- [ ] Cutthroat trout
- [ ] Garter snake

Black bear

Birds
- [ ] Western tanager
- [ ] Red-tailed hawk
- [ ] Pygmy nuthatch
- [ ] Gray jay
- [ ] Blue grouse
- [ ] White-tailed ptarmigan
- [ ] Red-winged blackbird
- [ ] Golden eagle
- [ ] Black-billed magpie
- [ ] Raven

Other Things I Saw
- [ ] _____
- [ ] _____
- [ ] _____
- [ ] _____
- [ ] _____
- [ ] _____
- [ ] _____

Dedication

For Quinn, Jaren, and Tony

Acknowledgments

My thanks to Riverbend Publishing for giving me a chance to write about one of my favorite places. I am also grateful to long-time Rocky volunteer Kathy Means for sharing her wealth of information about the west side, Jean Muenchrath and other National Park Service staff for helping make the book more interesting and accurate, and former Rocky rangers Vicki Cotton and Linda Austin (whose own red hardhat gets buzzed by hummingbirds) for providing support and ideas on my last research trip to the park. And for all the NPS employees and volunteers I worked with during my time at Rocky—thanks for helping make those years unforgettable.

About the Author

Julie Gillum Lue grew up in the Colorado mountains. She learned to love the outdoors and public lands, including nearby Rocky Mountain National Park. As a kid, she took her first real hike to Mills Lake! She graduated from the University of Colorado School of Journalism and also studied elementary education. After college, she worked for the National Park Service for about eight years, mostly in Rocky Mountain and Canyonlands national parks. She now lives in Montana, where she writes about family and the outdoors. You may find her online at julielue.com.

About the Photographer

Christopher Cauble grew up in Montana, where he began his passion for photography by exploring the mountains with a 35mm film camera passed down from his parents. After graduating from the University of Montana, he became a freelance photographer working mostly in Montana and Yellowstone National Park. His work has been featured in magazines and books, including *Yellowstone: A Land of Wild and Wonder*, *A Montana Journal*, and the popular children's book, *What I Saw In Yellowstone*. Cauble is also a nature cinematographer and his videos have been published on many national and international news sites and television programs. He lives in Livingston, Montana. His work can be found online at chriscauble.co and on social media.

What I Saw in Rocky Mountain
© 2019 by Riverbend Publishing
Text by Julie Gillum Lue
Photographs by Christopher Cauble, chriscauble.co
Published by Riverbend Publishing, Helena, Montana

Design by Sarah Cauble, sarahcauble.com

ISBN 13: 978-1-60639-112-9

Printed in the United States of America

1 2 3 4 5 6 7 8 9 0 VP 25 24 23 22 21 20 19

Riverbend Publishing
P.O. Box 5833
Helena, MT 59604
1-866-787-2363
www.riverbendpublishing.com

More What I Saw national park titles

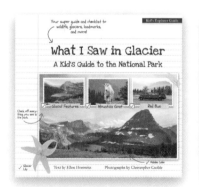
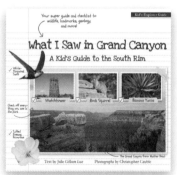

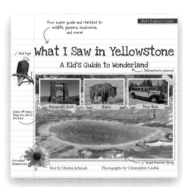

Available from your local bookstore or visit
riverbendpublishing.com or call toll-free 1-866-787-2363